Always Travel With Your Basket

A Self Development Book to Improve the Quality of Your Life

Sequel to Airbags and Starting Over, and Back On The Road Again

By: Karen Pivott

www.amazon.com/author/karenpivott

BY THE SAME AUTHOR

BOOKS ON KINDLE

NON FICTION

Airbags and Starting Over

Back On the Road Again
Always Travel With Your Basket

CHILDRENS FICTION

Birthdays at the Bay

Royce and Billy

FICTION

By Any Other Circumstances

Create Space Publishing
4900 LaCross Road
North Charleston, SC 29406
USA

First Printing, Create Space 2016

ISBN-9780473351403

Published in New Zealand

FOREWORD

I wrote this book because, since writing "Airbags and Starting Over" and "Back on the Road Again", I keep learning and experiencing great things and more, as I go along the exciting journey of life. I want to help **you** experience all the good that life has to offer.

Yes you deserve to receive good things. This book will help you change not just what you receive but who you will become in doing so.

That's right you will be working on the inside of you, but the world will see all the great things on the outside of you.

How cool is that?

Stop looking around the room. I am talking to you, so listen up and let's get started......

Contents

ACKNOWLEDGMENTS

My husband Alan, Jenni, Veronica, Lauren, Kathy and Kelly for their ongoing support. They have encouraged me and enabled my dreams to come true.

Special thanks goes to Muriel who did my proof reading.

I am truly grateful.

Chapter 1. What is the basket?

I have given this a little bit of thought. The whole concept of the basket arrived down the telephone line when I was discussing with a colleague a good thing that had happened for my husband.

"He has won first prize." I told her.

"It is about time you got something good. You deserve it. The tide is turning.   Now put your receiving basket out."

I have to confess I had never heard about a receiving basket before.

Many years ago I had kept a blessings box. A blessings box is where you put all the good things, all the good happenings, all the good situations, that you receive in real time as they happen.

It made me remember back to a time that, shall I say wasn't actually very full of blessings. In actual fact at the time I was directed to use a blessings box, I felt quite sure it would stay very empty.

I was wrong. As it turned out my blessings box got quite full over the course of that year.

This morning I found a basket, some coloured paper, and set to making small cards to fill in for our receiving basket.

What has really surprised me is all the things I have already filled out that have occurred this year.

Some of these things are actually quite big. My husband has been blessed, but so have I. I have received free things this year that have come about from quite unusual circumstances. I do have to say that even though the circumstances may be unusual everything is not only beneficial to me, but solving issues that I have asked a solution for previously.

Is this a coincidence?

Well if you've read my other books you will know already that I do not believe in coincidence.

I Believe in Divine Intervention. God in Us.

Be aware

At work the other day I overheard a conversation between colleagues who had all done a confidence course called "Outward Bound". This is a course of around ten days mainly working with the elements. The upshot of this course is that you get to know yourself. Your limits, your endurance levels, your coping strategies. You can then use these to reprioritize your life.

Out of this conversation another topic arose. The people who returned home and within a short time frame had left their husbands, wives and partners.

I asked questions about this and found that all three people had made changes to their lives as a result of this course.

Their tolerance levels had vanished. An awakening had occurred, they now had the strength, and the courage to make the change needed to better themselves and their families.

So common is this phenomena that a study has been conducted on it.

What does this have to do with a receiving basket?

Simply this. Sometimes when we know things are not right we look at the circumstances we are in, or are surrounded by, however we do not see that not only is there a better way to receive a better outcome. We can affect the outcome we need for ourselves and others. We can improve our lot so to speak.

Am I suggesting that we leave marriages or long term relationships to get a better outcome? Absolutely not, but if all other avenues for improving our relationships have failed then a decision needs to be made. To make decisions takes courage. Once a decision is made the way or means will be clear.

Decision Made

I made a decision once that I would speak up and make it very clear what I expected, and what action would be taken by me if things did not change. I wanted us as a couple to get back to where we agreed we would be when we got married.

We worked our way back to the expectations we had of each other, and the promises we made to each other and ourselves when we got married. We also added some things and deleted some others, because we recognized we were no longer the same people we were when we got married. We both had grown and evolved, and by extension now wanted different things.

I may add this did not happen overnight, but it has happened, and we now have a rich and rewarding relationship.

Not all things have to end to effect a change for the better.

A decision needs to be made though. If you need to effect change for yourself in any area of your life; if you feel you are treading water; keeping the peace; or tolerating the status quo; if you need to improve your situation, then make a decision to do so, and put that request into your receiving basket.

The way the improvement comes about may not be how you thought it would, but the result will be that you are in a better place than you were before.

This works in every area of your life and it works very successfully when you attach love to your request.

Attaching Love

So you are having an issue with someone and you need to be in a better place, how do you get there?

How do you attach love?

I think for me what I have learned, and I have touched on this in my other books as well, is that although we can be unhappy with our situation, we need to love people regardless. Not the situation, the people.

Does this mean we excuse what has happened or is happening?

NO!

What it means is that we love the person. The person we are not seeing as we need to at this moment. The person God intends the person to be. God loves us no matter what, and if we apply that principle to others nothing short of miraculous things will happen for us. Quite often unexpectedly. Sometimes a change outside of our situation brings the change we need for us to be in a better situation or place.

We live in a place where we have an all seeing God who sees, knows and hears everything. Yes everything, and in case you are wondering, especially our thoughts. If we have our thoughts ordered and disciplined, and we ask for change that will benefit us. If we love the person that we may think is responsible for our current situation, we don't hold onto negative thoughts about that person. When the good arrives don't be surprised. Be eternally grateful for the divine intervention that answered your request.

You asked for a better situation. You believed you would get it, because you knew it was what you needed. A better situation. You chose to do something about it when you made your original decision, to put your request into your basket. You worked to get your thoughts under control. You loved the person regardless.

You have received. No accident. No coincidence.

To outsiders it may look that way, but I assure you it won't be.

Things get put in place so you can receive, and they evolve over time, and often in unexpected ways.

I will give you an example.

I started in a new role in my job, and I had my own office. I lost my office and was put into a communal space. Something happened among the staff and I was relocated to my original office, which I now had to share with another worker. My colleague wasn't there often, but the space I originally had in that office on my own was now halved.

I was given a teaching space at the rear of building for my learners and that too was changed. I went into a different teaching space closer to my office, then that was allocated to someone else, and I ended up with no allocated teaching space. So my teaching resources were now in my shared office space and cramped doesn't describe the scene at all well. I began feeling sorry for my colleague who now had a tidy part of the office, and was confronted with an organized muddle every time she came into our workspace.

Now I don't want you to get the wrong idea about this. I loved working alongside this person, but I needed my own office.

I had been praying on the uncertainty and unsettling nature of all the shifting, and my working situation in general. Why? Because like many workplaces, we have movers and shakers in our workplace, and they often move and shake things on their agenda, for their benefit with little or no regard for other people. This was the continuing situation that was unfolding in our workplace. Then something happened I had not foreseen.

A person left. I am now in an office that only I use. It is perfect. Everything I need in the position I hold fits into that space and works well. Even the position in the building is perfect because I get low noise and very little interruption. The best thing of all is that my office has a name plate on the door. I share a teaching space behind me with another tutor and our schedules work out perfectly.

In the ten month lead up to all this I only saw the transitional disruption. I didn't see the end result. I didn't know what was happening or how I was going to get back into an office with a teaching space nearer to all the equipment and resources I needed to access. From the time I originally lost my office four years had elapsed.

Was I frustrated? Yes

Was I confused at times? Yes

Was I disenchanted? Yes

Did I stop focusing on having my own space with a teaching room attached? No

Did I have days when anger made an appearance? On occasion.

Through the whole process though I loved the

people anyway.

Is this a coincidence? No

Did this happen by accident? No

Did this happen by design? Yes

Did the workplace benefit? Yes

Did I benefit? Exponentially

THE LESSON I LEARNED: STAY FOCUSED AND LOVE WHATEVER HAPPENS

Chapter 2. Working with the elements

So what do I mean by this?

Working with the elements for a golfer could mean if you are in the rough keep putting.

Working with the elements in essence means that wherever you find yourself,   or whatever situation you are in, you work your way through the issue until you are clear of it, have completed it, have changed it or can leave in a better place than when you arrived.

Working with the elements also means that when you **are** in a good place, personal space or situation you acknowledge how good things are, give thanks for them, and work with others to spread the good around.

Good here doesn't just refer to money.

In my office I am in a good space, and I am able to help others more both learners and colleagues. This was not the case when all the disruption was occurring.

The one thing I am truly grateful for in my workplace right now is my office. My office allows people to come in and shut the door and talk through work things with me without interruption. This saves time so efficiency has improved. Sharing of resources happens more readily. There is more collaboration happening. Better results are occurring. Better communication is happening, because of where I am now located.

How are you dealing with the elements in your life?

Over time I have come to realise that we live in an adversarial society. Many people don't realise this.

From young children we are taught that by either manipulation or strength we get what we want.

What this means is that by the time we are

adults we are in competition with all of those around us who have been taught the very same thing.

Is it any wonder then, that when things come along which are challenging or problematic, we find ourselves all at sea.

The challenging or problematic things become elements in your life. The fun, the good, the joyous and the fantastic things equally become elements in your life.

So have a good hard think about how you are dealing with these elements.

My question for you here is, are you dealing with them at all?

If so are you completely happy with the outcomes you are getting? If not maybe ask yourself why not?

At the end of the day you are the one who knows the answer to these questions.

What I encourage you to do is to build on the good, be very clear about how you manage the challenging things, and set about getting yourself into a better situation.

Have you ever wondered why people who seem to have good luck, good fortune, good friends, are happy, and are people others want to be around, keep having those good things. This is not an accident. They keep having or receiving good things because every day they put the receiving basket out. They expect good things to arrive and they receive good things.

The exact same situation occurs when people find themselves in challenging situations. Have you ever wondered why someone you know always seems to be in the beginning, the middle, or coming to the end of a drama in their life?

The same rules apply. Whether it is consciously or subconsciously they are expecting the drama in their life.

Perhaps they were brought up with drama? Perhaps they have been approached, for help or advice, and have unwittingly become part of the drama. One thing I do know is this, it is very easy to become part of someone else's drama. I know this from personal experience, where I got caught up in other people's drama which cost **me** a great deal, those people not a whole lot, and it was not okay!

Even more unsatisfactory is watching from a distance and seeing them doing this to others, involving even more people. How? As I covered in my previous book 'Back on The Road Again' they are plausible. They groom people. Bring them in. Suck them dry and if people are lucky they get spat out.

They are people on reflection you realise you never should have met. They can cost you money, opportunity, professional growth and more.

They are skilled. You can try to tell people to be wary, but of course people are enamored with them by then.

You can be the ambulance at the bottom of the cliff, or you can be grateful that you have learned valuable skills in recognizing these people, and stay consciously away from them, using a lesson well learned to your advantage.

When you have been burned don't sugar coat it! Don't justify it. Be honest with yourself. Accept you have been duped, used, and manipulated. Make a conscious choice. Wash yourself off. Get up and walk away.

Easy?

Absolutely not.

Life changing?

Absolutely!

Moving on with new elements attached

So how do we get to use the new elements and attach them to ourselves exactly, and what are these elements?

They are the way you are now going to live your life with your eyes and ears open. You are going to see more clearly and recognize the elements for a) what they are, b) how they will affect you, c) whether you are going to allow them into your life or not.

The slips and temptations will be there but the more you are aware, the more likely you are to stay the course for a better outcome for you.

Keep checking. Do a visual check. Is what I am seeing what is happening? Is what I am hearing what is happening? Use what you see with what you hear collectively. Be actively looking and actively listening.

If someone is saying one thing, and their actions are doing something else, then you need to take notice and decide if what you are seeing is credible with what you are being told.

With the technological advances we are able to use this makes life a little more complicated, but remember this: Human Nature does not change.

When in doubt ask yourself this "Where is the evidence for this?"

How often is the story changing?

Who is jumping through hoops?

Who has the control?

You can trust me when I tell you that once the blinkers and ear muffs are gone, what you see and hear tells you the credible story. What you do with it is up to you, but I can assure you it is a lot harder to go along with something you can see is not right.

What's good about this? You can do a reboot or reset of the new elements that sit more easily and comfortably in your life and enjoy your life a whole lot more.

Will people leave your life? Probably. Will new people arrive into your life? Probably at some stage.

Will you be more at ease, rested, at peace, and healing? Without doubt.

Chapter 3. When you are sailing along and the wind changes

Yes just three short months into my new office and things going swimmingly well at work the proverbial hurricane arrived unannounced and with high velocity winds.

Restructuring in our workplace.

Surrounded by the fallout and not feeling too sure footed myself, I found my office being used by people that ordinarily I would say hello to on the stairs, or along the corridor as we got on with our respective jobs.

Nothing cements people like impending job losses. People who have been a problem in a workplace suddenly need to be protected as well.

I have been overwhelmed by the survival skills of my colleagues, and underwhelmed by the blame game the powers that be who are responsible for financial mismanagement have displayed to date.

My new found skills have been tested in ways I never thought I would have to experience, and we are just at the start of the process.

The most proactive thing I am doing to date for myself, is seeing myself coming through the hyperbole with myself, my clients and my job, or being better placed outside of the situation altogether.

I am holding firm to the belief that I and my colleagues will be better off. I feel and believe this will be the case, and am praying for everyone involved.

We are a week into the process and the shock has given way to anger. Working in an angry workplace is not an ideal environment to be in. Many of you reading this book will know all too well the unpredictable nature of finding oneself in a situation such as this.

There is also the unrealistic expectation that there will be business as usual.

The only business as usual for me at this point is the business of keeping myself in check, calm and available to others if they need some moral or practical support.

My clients are completely unaware of the changes and severity of our work situation. They are my priority of course, because I have a relationship with them to assist them to be better in their workplaces.

Yes I know the irony.

Well life is certainly not boring at the moment I can tell you that. It does though have an annoying habit of raising old wounds, and reactions to them, which do add to the challenge of it all. This is of course normal. The work I am doing on the tape in my head being muted or turned off is working overtime. This does take effort. Never the less it is working.

There is a lot of junk in my head space and I am pleased I can put it away into drawers at times. Some things do need to be dead locked so they never leave the drawer again, and I haven't found quite the right deadlock for that just yet. I **am** finding more sturdy drawers though, which is encouraging, because that means not all the drawers are opening back out at once.

Packing the drawers

Like all good collectors we have our favourite things that sit in a seldom used drawer. Some people have things at the back of a wardrobe. These are the things that you think about at the most inconvenient or pressing moments, pull out, dust off, try to use, or wear, even though they no longer serve the same usefulness or fit properly.

These are not things you want in your receiving basket, so put them back or dispose of them completely.

There will be lots of things to go into your drawers and like all drawers you need to rearrange them at times, empty them, or add some things to them.

If you want your receiving basket to become full of good, and even better things, a good place to start is packing the things you no longer need in secure drawers until you are ready to throw them out altogether.

For things to enter your receiving basket you have to make sure the basket is out, has room in it, and is on a stable foundation, so when all the good arrives the basket can hold it in place for you.

How do you ensure a stable foundation for

your basket?

You put away the things you no longer need to hang onto. You put them in a drawer or discard them completely.

What sort of things?

Dreams that are only dreams. Dreams that you don't really ever see yourself receiving or having.

Bad memories of something that was wanted, but has not arrived and you know deep down it won't.

Things that are in your thoughts, but you don't have an action plan for them.

Things you have received already and are truly grateful for. Acknowledge them in your basket and be grateful for them. They are your proof. These have arrived, have been used and are in your everyday life. Celebrate them. Keep using them and expect more to join them in your basket. Whatever you did, said, believed, expected for these will ensure your next delivery.

Never hold onto a delivery for fear it may leave you again.

It has arrived. Embrace it, use it and let it sit in your basket as a receipt.

This works for the good and the not so good. Sometimes when the not so good turns up we need to love and embrace that as well. Use it and let it go knowing we are in a better place regardless of its visit.

Once you have the receipt, be grateful, you can look at it often and be grateful as many times as you want, but you need to let the desire for it go because you have already received it. Now begin to concentrate on the next gift you want to receive.

There is so much misery in the world today because people hold onto what they are sent. They hold onto the good for fear of losing it. They hold onto bad for fear of what will happen if they let it go.

People give fear a life, and they end up not embracing life because fear becomes their life.

Don't believe me?

Remember a time when you didn't do something because you were afraid you would look foolish? Weak? A failure? You would be too successful and lose your friends?

Fear is what gripped you there.

An old soldier told me one day. "You are only in trouble if choose to do nothing when you have the opportunity to make a run for it. Some people may still be hit, but if you stay sat like a sitting duck you will all be roasted. I saw lots of that way too much of it. Fear paralyses. If there looks to be a way out, find it and keep moving till you are out. Nothing changed in the Second World War either. That's why I'm still here. I kept moving until I found a way out and it got me home."

For your receiving basket to be filled you need to have the courage to be thankful for what you have already and be courageous to ask for more, believe you will receive it, and know it is here for you already.

The guilt of receiving

When we receive something we have been wanting we are happy about it aren't we? I was asked this one day by a friend who had wanted a particular thing to happen for months and when it did happen, and she had it, she was not in the least bit happy about it. Because she wasn't happy about it at that point, she felt guilty she had received it.

Some of you will be able to relate to this scenario. It doesn't matter what the thing, person or event may be that you have wanted, and received. If you don't feel happy about that coming into your life, you have to be real.

It could be that the things that went with you
receiving something weren't what you had
believed they would be. It could be that a
person who looks great from a distance is not
so easy to work with, or know, when you are
in a one on one situation. It could be the
event, let's say a concert has been promoted
well, but the band or artist has just not
performed well on the night.

All these things can happen. They can
happen at any time to anyone. What holds
you in the disappointment of it all is guilt.
The feelings of guilt that well up as a reaction
to the disappointment that you are feeling.
You could feel let down, angry, or ripped off.

Your disappointment may also be with
yourself, the way you are performing in a new
role, or learning to use the new thing you now
have.

Things always look easy from the outside don't
they?

Some things you know you will never do, or
want to do. For me it is jumping out of a
plane with a parachute on. I admire people
who do it. I have even watched them do it.
Not for me though.

Then there are things I have wanted to do and
have done them to find out that yes I did it,

but I never wanted to do them again. These
are the 'Get up and walk away, and never look
back moments'.

Nothing wrong with these, you have had a go
and found out it is not for you. You may feel a
bit of guilt that you wasted some money on
the venture, but this kind of guilt doesn't tend
to last long you then focus on where your next
challenge may lie, or look for another
opportunity.

If you find yourself feeling guilty about
receiving something you may need to have a
good look at the WHY you wanted what you
now have, and be honest with yourself. Did
you want this to keep up with someone else?
To make a good impression perhaps? To
block someone else from having it?

If the why stacks up then you need to look at
how often you feel guilty when you get
something you have wanted.

Guilt, like all our emotions, can be a learned
behavior.

If you have been raised and told from a young
age that you don't deserve something this can
lead to feelings of guilt. Remember the tape in
your head? Turn it off.

If you have asked for something, believed you

would receive it and have received it, then there should be no guilt associated with it.

When we ask for something it is coming from a place within us. It is often something we feel we need, and our expectation is that it is going to make things better for us.

If it doesn't do that for us then we need to look at why that is. Do we need to do more to make it work for us? Do we need to add something to it to make it work for us? Do we need to revisit what made us think we needed that in our lives in the first place? Do we just not have the right information or teaching around what it is, in order to use it more effectively?

Just receiving something is not a 100% guarantee that it will work for us straight away.

Think about all the people who have studied and earned degrees, then left their college or university to get a job and are told "Why would I hire you, you have no experience."

I can see you nodding in agreement. Was it useless wanting the degree? Studying for the degree? Receiving the degree?

In that moment of rejection you could be forgiven for thinking yes, a complete waste of time, but learning is never a waste or a loss of your time. If you have learned and achieved it means you can learn, and that means learning how to gain the experience you need to get the job you want.

You may need a day job or regular job and do additional work in the field you want to work in. If it is what you have studied for and you get the opportunity to get the experience you will get there. It may not be the a, b, c process it looked like in the College or University brochure or advertising campaign, or even look like what the school guidance counsellor told you about that career, but if you want it, really want it, you will get there. If you decide you no longer want it then look for something else.

Your degree says this about you. You left school, and continued to study in this field, completed the study and achieved the degree.

What you do next is totally up to you. No one owes you.

A generation or two ago a degree meant something else. It meant that when you finished your degree you went into that particular type of job. That was necessary then because there were only so many places allocated for a degree, and those places were lined up with the availability of the jobs that were there in the workplace.

This is no longer the case. Is that your fault? No

We live in changing times. One of the things you could ask to come into your basket is an opportunity that will utilize my degree or what I have studied.

Something so much more amazing could be out there for you. You will never know that if you do not ask for it, or look for further opportunities.

Feeling guilty that you have a student loan, that you did all the work to get your degree, and that you don't have the job you wanted is detracting you from getting to the right job for you.

There are plenty of people who do have the degree, do have the job that goes with it, and every day they wonder why they still go to that job because that job is not meeting their needs.

We are people and people evolve. People grow. People change. People have the ability to evaluate where they are now, and where they need to be.

Guilt robs us of those processes. Like fear it stops us from moving forward. If you have got somewhere, or done something and it is not what you expected or is not working out, do not let guilt in. Information and redirection is what you need to be focused on.

I will say this, in my experience the biggest opening for guilt to arrive is the unrealistic expectations of others. Family members, friends, colleagues. Just because there are six lawyers in your family or group of friends, doesn't equate to you enjoying being one, even if you have trained for it. This is a good thing to remember because often unconsciously we put our unrealistic expectations onto other people and open a space for guilt to visit them.

What I have learned and am still learning is that it is all right to try something and decide it is not for you, walk away and get on with your life. There will be disappointments, but even they arrive for a reason.

Be clear about what you are asking for. Put your basket out and be ready to ask for and receive the next thing. Leave the guilt out of the mix altogether. You may find that what arrives next is the very thing that ticks all your boxes.

When you are getting up there in the numbers

I bring this subject up here, the age thing, because I have lived longer than some and not quite as long as some others. I am in that unique place where I have some experience and I am able to talk to those who have more experience than me. This is beneficial to me because I now have the maturity to listen and take on board what older people say. I respect they have lived through more or longer than I have, so have seen or been part of a different part of life to me. Why is this helpful?

Quite simply because you realise life goes in cycles. New things come along, and leave, trends appear, change, then disappear and we as a species evolve and move with all of it. That's what we do. That's who we are.

When someone offers you advice which you may not think is relevant to you, ask yourself this question. Why is this person telling me this? Is this even relevant to me? To my current situation? Is this something I should pay attention to for the future?

You see sometimes people come into our lives and tell us things that seem random in that moment. It is later we see their relevance. Remember that nothing is an accident. If someone is telling you something it is for a reason, what you do with that information is not their concern. They told you, and that is all they had to do.

Many years ago I was put into a professional group with a lady who told me lots of things and none of them helped me at the time. I was out of my depth and I was very tired, the result of these two factors was not a good combination.

A couple of years later I had to work with this lady again and I was dreading it. She told me lots and this time I wasn't struggling so much with my role. We had to do a presentation together and I remembered something she had told me two years prior. It just popped into my head and I used it to fill a gap between a question and an answer that was at the time elusive. This piece of information saved the day, the lady and the presentation. I have never forgotten that.

This lady and I became professional colleagues and good friends until she passed on from this life. I miss her but she left me an invaluable lesson. People, things, and information do not come to us for no reason. There is always a reason. As the years pass by I see the reason in all things much more clearly.

Often people will say "I just feel I have to tell you about....and I have no idea why that is." You will know why when the time is right and like me be very grateful you were told.

Age is also relevant when doing things with or for those who are younger. It is timely to remember that part of being young brings with it an optimism and enthusiasm that has no filter as life experiences haven't always been felt or observed.

Sadly for many this is not the case. There are the young among us who have experienced more than they should have, and therefore their contribution to life could be quite different to what some people may expect a young person would bring to the table.

We do however live in a society which is becoming increasingly dismissive of its older residents, and far too expectant of its younger residents. This in my view has put an unfair bias on both groups.

Young people still need time to amass knowledge, and as discussed in a previous book of mine, knowledge and information are not the same thing.

Likewise older people who have knowledge need time to adapt to changing norms such as technology, computers and how to use them, tablets, smart phones and the like. They are used to a medium of pen and paper, the written word, the spoken word. The means to communicate for an older person is quite different, and remember there were no spell checks to help in those days.

In my view there needs to be a fairer sense of respect between these groups. Each group has something unique to offer. Young, middle aged, older people in essence make up the whole. When the whole is working properly, seamlessly together, the collective community grows, and knows true harmony.

The idea that we need to be in constant competition, and getting attention is depriving us of working more cooperatively with an understanding that we can do better, individually, for our family and our community.

How do I know? Listen to the conversation of a young person as they talk about or refer to an older person. Is it complimentary, respectful or are they being rude, impatient, disrespectful?

Look at how an older person is treated on public transport. Are younger people giving up their seat or do they have the attitude that because they have paid for the seat it is theirs?

Do they laugh at older people or very young people and never offer to assist them? Do they take advantage of people?

What I have seen is a growing trend of people feeling and acting entitled to things that they have no entitlement to at the expense of others, and that in itself may be the minority of people across the spectrum. The impact of their behavior however is magnified by the lack of accountability from everyone else around them.

Remember if you say nothing or do nothing you are confirming their behavior is acceptable. If you are not confident to act when you are on your own, have some backup when you do act.

At all times though keep yourself safe. You don't have to be confrontational and turn things into a fight, sometimes a quiet word, or just walking away is enough to effect a change in behavior. Sometimes just not going along with the language, the attitude, the disrespect is also enough.

For things to change we have to work on changing ourselves, our expectations, our values and our behavior.

I never said that getting up there in the
numbers was managed by taking short cuts
now did I?

Chapter 4: Inspired love

Inspired love what is it?

It is love in action.

Yes it is in every one of my books usually scattered throughout the book, love or reference to it. Love is what does make the difference. Not selfish love but selfless love. What is selfless love?

When you do things out of, or for others with love.

How do we get there?

We must first love ourselves.

In Chapter Three we had a look at what happens when we go along in our lives and suddenly the wind changes.

You may be at that point right now.
Something has changed now or in the past
and you are still beating yourself up about it.
The direct result of that will be you are not in
the best possible place you could be. You may
feel alone, frustrated, angry, hurt,
disappointed, or seeing yourself as broken.
You may be just going through the motions of
your everyday life with the forced smile, being
polite, superficial conversations that keep the
world turning, but inside you are in pain.

When this happens even though you may still
be receiving good things you are not always
recognizing them as good things. Sometimes
when we feel like this we actually are receiving
more of the frustration, loneliness,
disappointments, hurt and situations which
bring about feelings of anger or angry
responses.

Recently a young person I know of who is a
lovely person by all accounts was confronted
with a situation that triggered events of the
past. This in turn evoked repressed feelings
and an out of character response which has
ended up in the courts. This young person is
remorseful, and genuinely sorry for their
actions, however the actions have occurred
and the consequences for them are real.

In light of what had triggered the action, had

the person responsible for the initial situation
been held to account in the first place this
current situation may not have occurred.

That said we are what we are, and in that
vein I want you to know that we have the
ability and capacity to change who we are ,
where we are, and where we are going and if
you are not in the best place possible right
now, you **can** get up and change that right
now.

Forgiveness

Hilary Clinton said in a recent interview that
she admired her mother because her mother
taught her it is not about when you fall down
it is about how you stand up and get going.
Further to that she added that forgiveness has
an absolute role in opening the doors which
allow us to move forward.

If you are in a place of unhappiness,
loneliness, hurt, anger, frustration or
disappointment in either yourself or the
actions of another person take a deep breath
and forgive yourself and/or them. Do it now.
Do it with your whole heart and let it go. Start
loving yourself right away. Believe in yourself
right away.

In my previous book 'Back On The Road
Again' I touch on the subject of injustice

because I, like many people, have experienced this first hand. I could have carried that, but I chose in that very instant to forgive all the people involved and lived from that moment on without them taking up space in my head. I did not dwell. Things continued to happen for a time afterwards, but once it was all finished up, it was completely finished up.

At the time I was feeling frustrated with myself. I had manuscripts written. I had rejection letters. I did not have books published. I had a shoe box full of hope waiting for publication. A friend of mine, as I explain in my previous book was ill and asked me if she could read something different. I gave her the shoebox just as I was going to dispose of it. She read the contents and handed it back. "You need to do something with these, they are too good to be in a shoe box"."

Around the same time my husband found a programme of Dr. Joe Vitale's called 'The Secret Mirror' which gets you to use a mirror to project yourself into the future to where you want to, or see yourself needing to be.

I was in a place of hurt and frustration and I wanted to be seeing my books published, so I looked into the mirror from a distance seeing my reflection and I saw my books published. I saw myself in a place of achievement, and I told myself how I had got there. Fantasy with projection? No.

I say no because deep within I knew what I had to do to get my books published. I had to find a publisher or another means to publish them. My husband found me the means. Amazon.com Kindle Direct Publishing.

I was in my mid-fifties what did I know about publishing? Absolutely nothing so I set about finding out.

Now I am not a marketing person who has chosen to write for extra cash. I am a writer who needs her words to get out there in the hope they will educate, help and entertain people depending on the genre I am writing.

At that time I realised I had to rewrite my work to meet the format requirements of the electronic publishing platform.   Right there I was learning. Learning new terminology. Learning new techniques from a book step by step. It was daunting. No I did not find it easy. My husband was supportive, and gave me the space I needed to get my head around something completely new.

While I was learning all these new things I started looking in my mirror and seeing things getting easier and easier, seeing my published books increasing.

Less than six months later my first book was published on the Kindle platform.

One of the benefits of living for a while is that you get to see a lot of things. One of the things I have seen is that what people tell you to do that looks and sounds reasonable NEVER works out for everyone. I have taken a different path to enable my dreams to come true. I have found that path because I have chosen to look for it with my eyes wide open. It may sound fantastical to some, but so did talking to someone on a telephone once.

Looking back I can now see that my decision to forgive allowed me to move on to where I needed to be. All the things I needed to do became visible. Were they there already? Yes, but I wasn't looking for them.

Remember this, we come into this world on our own. We leave on our own. We are cellular, emotional beings. We arrive with everything we need to make it on our own.

I have a strong faith, I am not denying that, but that too is because I am open to it. I choose to believe. I choose to accept that even when what I, or others, may deem to be

impossible and unseen in the first instance
does become real when you ask for it, and
believe, it does arrive.

My published books are proof of that.

Now I have to learn how to sell them which is
what I am trying to do while I write this book.

You are never too old to learn, so the learning
continues.

Documentaries

The Backstreet Boys I read when flicking
through the TV book. I took a breath and
went back to the page. There was to be a
documentary of this group screening on
Thursday night that week part one of two.
Now I am not a Backstreet Boys fan. I have
heard their music over the years, but that's
about it. I remember at their height they were
marketed as a phenomenon. They saturated
media around the world across all its forms.
TV coverage. Radio. Magazines. Newspapers.

I set the tape to record the programme
thinking that I would flick through just to see
where these men were now. Twenty years on.

My initial thought was I would be doing more
skipping than watching the documentary. I
had thought it was to be a reality TV type

programme from the promos that had been aired over the week.

Now I will say here when I get it wrong I tend to do a good job, and this is one of those occasions.

Was the documentary emotional? Yes

Did it have melt downs and arguments? Yes

Did it have tragedy? Yes

Trust issues? Yes

I watched both episodes in their entirety. I am not a fan of the group itself, however I was very impressed with the young boys who have become men and forged a default family unit over the last twenty years in a loving supportive way. I genuinely mean this.

I have never met the "boys". I have worked with youth though, and it never ceases to amaze me how we place our most vulnerable in precarious situations blinded by the big prize mentality.

Love in action

The reason I have brought the documentary up is to tell you what has been demonstrated throughout the documentary. Love in action. These boys have gone from the high five, hug, slap on the back, we did a great performance/we nailed it demonstration of camaraderie, to a thank you for the last twenty years, congratulations, hugs and shared admiration for each other born out through years of sticking together, loyalty, trust, accountability and good old fashioned love for one another. That is the hero of this documentary, of their story, the unabashed love they have for each other, individually and collectively.

Let's not forget they can all sing. How do I know this when I am not a fan. Two reasons. One I am not tone deaf. Two I had the opportunity to see them on the television once singing without any musical accompaniment and they are extremely good, with or without instruments in the mix.

They work hard. They practice a lot, so they have honed their musical skills, but at the core of it, they love to sing, love to perform, and love performing together.

As I have said many times. Love is a tangible thing. It is real. It moves people.

These people, like many others, have forged a bond through situations and circumstances that have arisen in their lives. They have the integrity to own the not so good things, deal with them and carry on, as well as acknowledge the good things and good people who they have happened across through their lives and say thank you to them.

The everyday people

We all know people who have a story of perseverance and achievement. These are everyday people. With the way our lives are being opened up and scrutinized we forget that people in bands, on television, and all manner of other areas are still people. These people had everyday lives before they were thrown into the spotlight.

We often judge people on the perception that is sold as fact.

Take a woman who is having an affair with a married man. A celebrity. Because the married man is in the public eye once the affair is out there, so too is the woman and the wife. Now the media may focus their attention on the woman at the heart of the affair, or the wife, or the husband, but at no time do we get to see the three people involved falling over. We don't have the facts. We have the projection of the perception playing out on our screens and across our airwaves.

A good case in point was a series Jamie Oliver did when he went to Italy. His wife was to

meet him there in one week. She was upset.
This was all filmed. The next day the
headlines were: "Friends of friends say Oliver
marriage to end." All a fabrication, a ruse to
sell newspapers and magazines. Who keeps
buying into this destructive cycle? The people
who keep buying the newspapers, magazines,
or those now reading these articles on the
internet where other forms of advertising
revenue is raised.

How much love is being circulated when we
are distracted by this?

Just something to think about!

Chapter 5. The joy of being involved or around when others receive

Yes the receiving basket doesn't just work for yours truly. In recent years I have seen many colleagues change jobs, change relationships and be all the happier for it. Winning competitions, achieving qualifications and receiving all manner of wonderful things that they have wanted.

In every case the timing has been perfect. In every case the timing has not been when the person thought things would happen. For some people it happens much more quickly than they thought it would, and they feel overwhelmed or not quite ready. For others it happens exactly at the right time, and they accept and embrace it for still others it takes a lot longer than they expected, and sometimes that means they walk away from it, or go ahead with it with some resentment.

I have been waiting for something for a long time, and I am focusing on the receiving of it like I actually have it already, and am grateful for it. I am not focusing on waiting for it to arrive. I cover this in my previous book ' On The Road Again'. I can do this because I have observed over time that the timing is perfect.

If something comes to you more quickly than you anticipated that does not mean that it is too soon.

If something takes a long time to arrive, that does not mean you don't deserve it.

Keep your receiving basket out and keep collecting and making a record of what you have received. When you receive the last small thing you need, the big thing you have asked for and believed you will receive arrives. Where is my proof for that? Sometimes we need the little things to be in place first.

I myself have realised this. My Dragon Speak arrived after my accident when I couldn't use a keyboard. I was given my writing desk unexpectedly, which is a desk you stand at to use. Then several months later my computer arrived, and a set of drawers. Currently I am writing in a room between two beds and items being stored. Have I given up on my writing room? Of course not, I have everything now to go into it and I am thankful for my writing room, just as I was thankful for my standing desk, my own computer and a set of drawers to store things neatly in. I even have the artwork for my writing room, some of which is on the wall in my current temporary writing space.

Every day I am grateful for these things because it makes writing in my own space a reality.

I am bringing this up here because sometimes when we see others receiving we become frustrated, disenchanted, jealous even, that they are receiving and we are not.

Here is what I have learned. The more grateful and happy you are for their success, achievements, or good luck and I mean genuinely grateful and happy for them, the more your receiving basket will start to fill up too.

Never be or feel unhappy when someone else has received something that makes them happy. Happiness is contagious. The more

you are infected by it, the more happiness you
receive in your life.

When something good or great comes into
your life, don't be surprised when people
around you are happy for you, accept their
happiness for you and watch the enjoyment of
whatever it is you have received grow inside
you.

Whenever a family member, colleague or
friend wins something big or small I am truly
happy for them. We don't have the right to
dampen someone's good fortune, or
achievements. In fact we owe it to ourselves
to be encouraging of their next step. Often
when we achieve or win something it brings
unexpected things or expectations with it, and
to meet those additional arrivals takes
courage. Being happy for someone when they
receive helps them. Remember when you
receive you often receive more than you
thought you would, and sometimes there is no
game plan in place for that.

If you know someone has received something
they have wanted and they are finding it is not
as straight forward as they thought it would
be to deal with, offer to support them through
the process and continue to be happy for
them.

I am bringing this up here because we often only see the first part of the process,   then we may see the person later on and they appear to be miserable or ungrateful. This only happens when something unexpected has arrived as part of the receiving. Take an overseas holiday. You buy a product and go into the draw to win a trip for two for seven days on an island. You win the competition and you are very excited. Then you find out the promoter has changed the dates you can take the holiday. You can't redeem the holiday for cash. You can't give the holiday to someone else. Now the holiday you have won is an issue, because you are unable to get leave for that time of year. You enter into a process of trying to salvage your holiday. There could well be people around you who didn't want you to win the holiday in the first place. Wouldn't you rather have someone in your corner who can support you through this change? I would. When things change unexpectedly that too can happen for a reason so there is usually a way to resolve things.

New starts

There are times when you really want something and it is a big something like a new job or career, starting a new business venture, buying a new home, shifting to a new location or a mixture of the above.

Many times people you know will mention in passing that they would like to do... or they would like to live....., and you may agree with them or state what you might like to do as well. Time passes and these people start doing exactly what they had mentioned they would do to you, and you are still exactly where you were.

This has happened to me recently. Friends of ours who have wanted to move house for a couple of years sold their house and moved to a new location in walking distance of everything they need, and I am absolutely thrilled for them. The old me would have spent time feeling hard done by or hacked off that they had shifted before me.

Then just this week news of a family member selling their home and shifting to a coastal town also reached us, and I am equally thrilled for them. They have been dreaming, talking and planning this move for years and now it is in the process of happening.

So two couples close to us. One couple have shifted and are very happy in their new home and new environment, and are making new friends, and the other couple who have sold their current home and looking at property in their chosen area as I write this.

Where am I? A lot closer to my move. How do I know this? Quite simply because the people I know have either moved or are on the move and we all saw our moves clearly so of course I'm excited, who wouldn't be.

This is why it is so important to be happy for others they are lighting the way for you. They are showing what is possible. Don't be envious. Be grateful.

Enjoying the gains we have already made

Yes shifting to be nearer our family in our country home is on my agenda, but I have achieved a lot of momentous things on the way to there.

I have realized the two story mansion which looked great in the brochure was actually not so practical for someone who has balance issues and a husband whose knees have seen better days.

The Beef Block I wanted to wander about is not on the flat and since my accident not such a sensible choice either.

My current thinking is far more practical and more me. I will be comfortable and happy so what more can a woman want.

There is something to being comfortable it brings a depth of contentment and enhancement to one's life.

Do I like flashy. Oh yes! I not only like it I love flashy, but I am just as happy without it.

I have made gains in the last five years that I would never have thought possible. Writing and publishing my books obviously, but they are not the only things I have achieved. I have sat and passed exams. I have helped hundreds of people. I have put the past to bed and no longer spend time on the future, it is not here yet. I project what I would like it to look like, yes, I put myself in it, but 1 don't worry about it.

I am much more centred and focused on how to maximize the now and be effective in my personal and professional life.

I am now in a much better place for my new start and I believe this is the key to receiving it. I am not in charge of the how or the timing, but what I do know and what I have observed is that when the means and the timing line up it will be seamless.

Being the right person in the right place at the right time every time

I recently completed a Master Life Coaching Certificate with Dr. Steve G. Jones and in it he said something I had never given conscious thought to. It is fine to be in the right place at the right time but to be truly successful you need to be the right person in the right place at the right time. How do we do this?

Ask for it every day and enjoy the shift in your situation.

Bob Proctor talks about this a lot. Essentially to be in the right place at the right time every time you need to desire it and expect to be there every time.

Not fluke it. Expect it.

Think about when you received something. An award perhaps. There were lots of people up for the Award and you are the person who received it. How did you feel before you received it?

Did you expect it? Was there a thought in the back of your mind that it was your turn to receive it?

Often we have little thoughts or feelings like this, and then we, for any number of reasons, talk or think ourselves out of receiving it.

That's right. "Mary is bound to get it again she is so lucky."

Really? Well Mary probably got it again because you just handed it to her.

What if you had said or thought "I am so ready to receive this thank you." Or "Well it is my turn to receive it this week." Really meaning it and being thankful.

Now this may not occur right away but the more you think, speak or act this way the more likely you are to become a receiver.

And remember ask to be the right person in the right place at the right time every day, and you will see things that you normally miss, or something will come along that you need and you will be right there to receive it.

The first thing I do after I have received something and written it on the card and put the card in my basket is to get a blank card out and have that sitting in my basket ready to fill in. I expect to receive something else and I can tell you my basket is filling up with things that I have never received before.

One of the amazing things that have happened on this journey is the people who have

supported me, or started to speak to me.
These people I have been around or known as
a colleague, but we have never really talked
and it is nice.

Even my Doctor with whom I have had a
rather reticent relationship with in the past.
Surprisingly now we have productive
conversations when I see him. To be fair I
don't put the blame for past communication
issues totally on him, I tend to go to the
Doctor when I am unwell, thankfully that is
not often, but I am not at my best on these
occasions and I don't go for chit chat.

The current focus of giving the patient all the
information is good, but at times
overwhelming. I recently had influenza and
was very ill. I was given information on the
complications that can occur and what to look
out for and what actions to take in the event
that....then I was told about the statistics of
having those issues 4%, then the 27%, and
asked what happens to the other 69%? I was
informed they usually come through all right
but are tired for a period afterwards. My
response was that I do not have time to be in
the 31% so I will rest up and expect to come
through it okay.

Now if that was me, and I was the Doctor I
would have started with the 69% and then

explained for a smaller number of people they may experience... The doctor of course has a different role. He needs to get his patient to recognize the worsening symptoms so they seek further prompt medical intervention if needed.

It is all in the how we tell the story at times, and what the outcome for the person needs to be. For a patient it needs to be for that person to be treated and get well.

Frankly I impressed myself by being able to work out the 69% I just wanted to be home in bed feeling sorry for myself. Looking at this in a different context the 69% gave me a focus away from feeling sorry for myself and a goal to rest, get well and get back to work.

Normally if I was a bit under the weather I would carry on. I work with people every day though, and even I know when to do the right thing by myself and others in the area of health.

Doing right by yourself

So being the right person, in the right place at the right time every time, has a lot to do with doing right by yourself as well.

You need to be in the right head space. You need to be available. You need to expect

something and you need to be ready. You
need to be accepting and most of all you need
to be persistent.

Just because you are the right person, in the
right place, at the right time, every time does
not mean you win every time, but often you
may see, hear or become better off by having
just been there.

A little while ago I went somewhere to pick
something up and there was a mix up. What I
had purchased had inadvertently been given
to someone else. What I had purchased then
had to be reordered, however something else
arrived which was similar. It was larger and a
bit more expensive, but they asked if I would
be happy to take that instead. When we got it
home it was perfect.

This being in the right place at the right time
every time doesn't always work out how we
think it will, but we are always better off in
one way or another. If we are not better off,
then it is not the right time for us.

Chapter 6. Keeping your mind actively on the job

Yes this is the hardest thing of all to do. I can hear you now thinking we have just read a whole lot about this and that is true but doing it every day?

Doing it while you enjoy your chores, your ups, your downs?

You know nothing focusses your thoughts, your mind, your attitude, your outcomes like a bad situation, bad attitude, or expecting something bad to continue in your life.

When we are sailing along happily we get very sloppy. Oh yes sloppy. We often forget that we are happy because we did the work to get happy. The mind work. The expectation. The asking. The Believing. The Accepting. The Gratitude. Yes we just start taking it all for granted instead of focusing on other good outcomes we could be focusing our mind on.

This doesn't just have to be for ourselves. If you truly have everything you want for now and are blessed with having more than you need in an area of your life such as time for example it is perfectly okay for you to give some of your time to help others.

Let me tell you what happens when you do this. Immediately you find something that is needed that you can focus on which will result in something good for others.

How do I know this?

How did you get the spare time in the first place?

Oh yes and the bonus of this is you do not have time to let the bad, negative, defeating thoughts to revisit, start playing and take hold.

Will they pop up? Of course they will. So why bother then? If you are focused on good for yourself or others it is the best fire extinguisher you can have to stop the bad thoughts, attitudes, or negative behavior from having any place in your life.

You can literally snuff out the life of the negative invasion, because focused good thoughts will prevail if you let them.

That's right we are right back to the personal responsibility and personal accountability.

It starts with you. It ends with you. Think about your ending and make it a good one.

The mess ups

There are going to be times when you mess up. I am extremely good at this myself and tend to mess up in spectacular fashion.

What I have learned is the more spectacular the mess, the better and more quickly the recovery phase occurs.

When you mess up, the faster you own it and put it right the better for everyone, and that is especially the case for you. There may be a longer term cost for you, but remember who was it that messed up?

Now there are times when the mess is not of your making. You become part of the mess and the mess may not be resolved as you would like. Remember this, God knows what is happening. In these situations when you

feel yourself in a war, or being put upon,
forgive yourself for those feelings, and the
people who you think are in the wrong, and
ask for a good outcome. Believe you will
receive a good outcome and accept the
outcome. You see there may very well be
something fantastic for you that you know
nothing about right in the middle of the mess.
Something that you will be in a position to
take up once the mess ends.

I am supporting people right now who are
going through mess and none of us have
created the mess. So far everyone who is now
out of the mess is better off. The way they got
out of the mess has been as unexpected as the
mess itself. I have no idea why I am still in
the mess but I am learning things about
people and their behavior that has already
resulted in good for others, so it is not a waste
of my time being there at the moment. It is
unpleasant at times and very unsettling,
however my focus is not on the mess. My
focus is firmly on my good outcome when I too
am liberated from it.

Liberation

The Concise English Dictionary has this
definition for liberty.

'The state or act of being free.'

Being free can be a conscious act. Nelson Mandela is the perfect example of this. He was imprisoned but never allowed himself to be defeated, in his mind he was free.

There are times when quite unexpectedly something will happen, or someone will come along, and these chance encounters enable us to know we can be free of the messy situation even when we are still in the mess.

This happened to me the other week. I had been working alongside an agency for many years and last year due to our changes and theirs, I wrote to them and suggested that the relationship between us end.

Now remember this was last year when things were going well and there was no mess on the horizon.

Out of the blue I got an appointment to meet up with a person in this agency. A person who had worked there, but had been gone from there for some time and had now returned.

I thought that as an agency they did need to know the changes to the service we could now offer their clients so I went along to the meeting.

By the time I left that meeting I knew that my

current action plan of focusing on the good
was working. It was working because the
person who I had just met with told me why
she had left and then returned. Her journey is
closely aligned with current situations that
people I know are facing.

Her experience and her outcome has given me
hope and confidence that when the mess,
whatever it is, is not created or initiated by
you, and you don't buy into it, the resolution
and outcome is always better than you ever
could have hoped. Remember this, if not now,
then at some time in the future the truth
always comes out.

The truth was revealed when this lady left and
the person who bullied her out did not have a
sounding board any longer to give her the
knowledge or the skills to do the job she was
employed to do. That person then left and the
business found that they had lost the
experience of the worker they had not
supported.

Reports are wonderful things. They can give
facts and help grow a business. They can also
be used to manipulate information when there
is an agenda in play.

The business rang this lady and offered her,
her old job back. Fortunately for her she was

working somewhere else and enjoying being out of the mess of that workplace.

Then her job finished with the business being closed.

Again her former boss contacted her and they have come to an arrangement which is working well for everyone.

The boss has learned a lot too.

I have covered this before, if in doubt ask "Where is the evidence for that?"

If you are being told you are not up to the mark, under performing, don't know what you are doing and you are still getting the right outcomes for your job, or your kids, or your family, or your husband, ask yourself "Where is the evidence for this?" If the evidence is that you are delivering, you are performing, then start focusing on a good outcome for yourself, and expect one.

The earlier you do this the better position you are putting yourself in.

Your gut will already have been sending signals so don't ignore them.

Spiritual armour is the most effective armour in the world, and we can access it for good twenty four hours a day seven days a week.

If you feel exposed, start getting yourself
protected.

Chapter 7. Believing in your dream

Many successful people will often say the same things.

I knew it would happen. I believed I would find a way. I made lots of mistakes. I always wanted to do this.

We have all heard these comments before. We may have said them ourselves at times, but here's the thing, when your dream is not visible in your everyday reality, it is a lot harder to believe in it.

Even people who have a plan in place and are actively working towards their dream may become bogged down in the everyday tasks they are doing, to the extent that they lose sight of their dream.

Making your dreams visible is a learned behavior.

Visualisation helps with this, as do meditations, affirmations, and vision boards. Time in prayer also helps.

Do you know what learning style you have? If you do, then you can use that, to drive your dream on.

For example if you are an auditory learner make a recording of your dream and listen to it. Talk to yourself about it.

If you are a visual learner have pictures of your dream in places you often are, and look at them daily.

If you are a reader then write down everything you can think of that is in your dream and read it three times a day.

If you are a kinesthetic learner, a person who likes to do or touch, actively seek out information to do with your dream.

Look it up on the internet. Make a resource folder up about it. If it is a particular style of house for example get a brochure from the Real Estate Office or download a picture complete with plans. Go for a drive and look at the gardens around your house. Take note of where the house sits on the section.

Whatever your style use it to make that dream a real thing for you. Once that dream feels real it is much easier to work towards it.

Going to, not running from: there is a difference

I have touched on this before with the fear factor, but in this instance when you have a dream and you want that dream to become your reality, you need to be honest and ask yourself why you want it.

Now take a large house. If your dream is to live in a large house to show everyone how successful you are, then you actually have two goals and will need to prioritise those.

If you want to live in a large house because you want to have people to stay with you in comfort, and have lots of room for everyone, and you are currently living in a one bedroom apartment, then you will make steps to get to your large home.

Can you see the difference? In both cases you are moving towards your goal and usually this takes more than one step.

If you are in the apartment then you have to

source a house.

If you want the flash large house to show off
your success then you have to first be a
success.

Now moving towards a goal is crucial but why
you are moving there is just as important.

If you are wanting to have a large house so
you have more places to hide or take refuge in
because you are living in fear of someone, that
is not moving towards a goal in this context.
That is going to a place out of fear and
anyone who has been, or is in that situation,
will also know that at the end of the day, there
is no house big enough to hide in when you
give life to fear in any situation.

Now living in the large house without fear and
in safety that would be a more appropriate
dream to have.

Your dream does not have to be singular. It
can encompass everything. It is the priority,
the order of importance which counts.

Going towards, means you plan and see the
better place you are in, and keep looking and
moving forward while you get there.

Running from, means you are always looking
back, and when we look back we lose our

focus for the road ahead.

The dream who owns it?

Very often we have a dream and we may mention it to someone else and immediately one of two things happen. It is criticized or praised.

Many times the criticism comes in the form of chucking off at your dream, or being sarcastic about it. "I'm sure we would all like to have that."

"Really what makes you think you can do that?"

"Why on earth do you want that?"

Many times the praise will be superficial.

"Good on you. When you have your millions don't forget you told me first."

"That's a great idea. I will be calling you when you pull that off, and you can help me with some stuff."

Now people aren't saying these things to be mean. They will be surprised or shocked at what your dream is.

But here is something I want you to think about.

Whose dream is it?

It is your dream.

Who owns the dream?

You do.

Who is responsible for working towards it?

You are.

There are times when you will share a dream with someone, so in that case you will have to work collectively to see that dream come true. So long as each person involved stays focused and clear on what is needed, and takes ownership of the dream the result will be the same.

Be disciplined. If you have a dream and you want to tell someone about it choose the person carefully.

With my writing I told a colleague who kept me accountable to my dream.

"How are you progressing with your book this week?"

There were some weeks I had made no progress at all, but she never said you won't ever realise your dream, she would more likely make comments such as, " now that is out of

the way you will have another good run at it."
"Would you like me to look at what you have
done around that piece of writing and we
could talk about why you think it's not
working."

"You are working full time and have other
commitments you are allowed some time to
yourself."

Non-judgmental, non-threatening,
encouraging comments.

This person also became a supporter of my
dream to study and pass exams which I have
achieved and what a great morning tea we
shared when I took my certificate along to
show her. She was not in the least bit
surprised I had passed but did say, " You sat
the exam without needing to talk to me first.
That is real progress. I am so proud of you."

Our morning tea spilled into the lunch slot.

If you don't have someone to share your
dream with that is also fine and works better
for some people.

Write down your dream. Or make a recording
of it. List all the steps you need to take and
the things you need to do, to make your
dream your reality, and be accountable to
yourself.

You know sometimes with dreams it is all in the timing, and sometimes the time frame is longer than we would like, but always without exception the time delay, or expediency is for our benefit so don't question it. Just go with it.

Remember it is your dream. You have put it out there. You are accountable and responsible for working towards it, but that does not mean you can't accept help along the way. Unexpected help or circumstances often is what pushes your dream home.

I have over the years had many dreams, and what I have learned is the size of the dream is not important.

A small dream can take longer than a big dream.

A big dream can come about very quickly.

What they have in common though is the actual belief that the dream will happen for me.

If the dream is for others and they don't want it, then you are wishing for others. It is a wish for them.

They have to want the same dream for it to be real for them.

No matter how small or how large, own your dreams, make them work for you, and never be afraid of wanting more or too much.

We are not here to be miserable.

We need to have aspiration. We need to inspire ourselves, succeed and show others there is a better life for us, and we can have it.

Imagine it, then believe it is yours, and make it come to you.

Dreaming and believing is relieving stress in your life because you are focusing your energy on a better outcome for you. This is empowering, and you are empowering yourself by believing in your dreams.

When your dream does arrive be extremely thankful and grateful for it.

Chapter 8. When we complain

Please don't sit there and tell yourself you do not complain. We all complain. I am no exception. It is human nature. It is something we learn to do when we are young. It is enforced when we get someone into trouble because of it, or we get a lot of attention at the time because we are complaining. We have a listening ear which is allowing us to complain. Yes even when we are told by someone, "Stop complaining." It is enforcing the right we may feel we have to complain.

Why do people complain? Often when we are younger it is to get what we want.

Often when we are older it is a behavior we revert to when we are hurt or frustrated or dare I say it bored, and not appreciating all the good things we have to be grateful for. We become complacent and complacency leads to dissatisfaction. You can see the pattern can't you?

When we are in stressful situations a great distraction is to complain about the very people who are in the mix at the time.

It could be a nurse who spoke harshly to someone or appeared to be too rough with our loved one.

A new Manager whose management style is so different to what we are used to we take everything they say as a slight.

The people who are high achievers and always winning awards, receiving praise, and always in your face, can appear to do no wrong. Yes those people, we even complain about them. "Imagine living with them they are so full of themselves."

Really? We don't actually know these people, so how could we possibly know what they are like to live with. Exposure is one thing. Knowing people is something else entirely.

Working with people is one thing. Living with them is something else.

When we start complaining about the people

in our lives we need to get ourselves in check.

Yes even when we know in our gut something is not right. Even when we have proof something is not right or not adding up, especially then we need to keep ourselves in check and our thoughts on all the good that is happening in our lives regardless and love those people anyway.

Ensuring we receive all our good things

I have said it many times across all my books in many different ways, to receive our good we must focus on all the good things that we have received already, whether we are waiting for some of them to physically show up or not.

We must be focused all the time.

Complaining doesn't necessarily stop us receiving, but why would you receive something if you keep complaining about something you have received already?

There are times when you receive something you want. Let's take a job. You have left a job and go to a new job. You love your new job. It is everything you've always wanted. You are doing well in your new job when you decide you want to be promoted.

You apply for a promotion and you are

unsuccessful. You feel aggrieved, frustrated.
You have been in the job some time now and
proven yourself in your role. You want to do
more, be more in that company.

You start to complain about the person who is
in the role you applied for. Just a few isolated
things here and there at first. Then the
person does something that is not accepted by
those around them and people start agreeing
with what you have said. This fuels another
round of complaining. You are now actively
seeking things to complain about, while you
are asking to be relocated to either another
area of work or another job altogether.

Now let's break this down. You are in the job
you asked for. You are doing well in the job
you asked for. Did you ask for this job and go
straight to it or was there a waiting period?
The job you had previously, was that a job you
asked for or did you take that job while you
were waiting for the job you really wanted to
come up that you are now in?

Do you have a pattern of complaining when
you get the job you want?

When we are in the job we want, we are
responsible for doing our very best in that job
and that is all.

What other people do in their jobs is not our

business. If we see them doing things that make us feel uneasy or concerned we need to keep those things to ourselves and ask for a solution that will be beneficial to ourselves and our colleagues.

I have lived this throughout my working career and many times in the past I complained because I got myself so worked up. Let me just say this. Complaining does not change other people, what it does do is take your energy away from what you need to do, which is continue to be grateful and focus on your solution.

We do not know what is in a person's heart. We do not know why someone else is doing what they are doing. The one thing we do need to do is decide what we want and continue to work towards that without complaining.

How do we do that?

We take ourselves to task when we start to think negatively about those we may complain about, and hand those negative thoughts over to a power far greater and wiser than us.

I ask for forgiveness straight away. Yes I do have the odd slip if I am being totally honest with you, but they are getting further apart these days.

Be aware, take heed of what you are observing or being told. Be informed but do not complain about it.

Forgive and love them anyway. Then get on with your day. Do not inflame the situation. Do not try to correct the situation. Trust that you will come through what is happening and be in a better place or situation anyway.

This is not easy. I have come through this very scenario in three of the workplaces I have worked in over the years and the common denominator in all of them is change. When systems or compliance change occurs, restructuring, or personnel changes in a role, or enters a workplace, the change is very often a catalyst for difference, and difference can bring stress.

What I have learned is, it is easy to have an idea of what something is going to be like, but once you get there it tends to look quite different, and with the best 'can do' attitude in the world there will be some things you still need to learn to be effective in the role, and if you challenge people through that phase there will be consequences for you', because they often feel threatened.

If you are genuinely trying to be helpful and your help is not received well, just stay in your role and keep doing that well, while you think about what you need to do and where you need to be next.

At all times keep yourself safe.

Sometimes the people around you start leaving and going to different workplaces, and they look much better when you see them in the street. Talk to them. Ask them why they left. You will find a pattern if there is one. If not maybe you need to look at why you are feeling so uneasy and ask for patience and guidance yourself. If you are no longer meant to be there, and you are focused on a good outcome for yourself, you will get there much sooner if you are not complaining.

You know sometimes we are not left in a situation for our own benefit initially, we are there because others need support as well and when the time is right we get an amazing solution so if you are a complainer please start changing that today.

Be excited wonderful things are happening every day, to make your wonderful happen. Stop complaining, be grateful and give thanks for everything you have and continue to receive every day.

Give thanks for the small things, they grow into amazing things, over time.

Chapter 9. The small things

I have been blessed recently with an amazing group of people coming into my life. I would not ordinarily have met these people they move, live and work in different situations to me. So you may wonder how did I meet them.

Well I can tell you. It came from a need they had. They wanted to learn how they could do more with their money and requested a financial literacy course.

I had never run one of these before as such. Budgeting I had done but what these people wanted was different to that. It would be fair to say that I was more than a little apprehensive. Money tends to trigger all sorts of things for people, and these particular people did not have a lot of means, however they wanted to do more with what they had, and learn how to have money without stress.

Exactly, now you know why I was apprehensive, but the request had come from them, they had a need to be met, and I bit the bullet and put a course together.

I will say here I had arranged for speakers to come in and share their expertise with the group as well, which did not always work out the way I had intended, but all I will say to that is no learning is a waste, even when it is the Tutor learning what to do or not to do again.

Adding to the mix

The group was small to begin with but their enthusiasm was boundless and they began to bring others into the group which doubled to a very good number.

Each person participated which, if I am honest when they first arrived, I could not see happening, but there is magic in the air so to speak, when these people are together.

So with our differences in play we began and continued and to my surprise this has been the highlight of my year to date. Not only have they exceeded their own expectations, they have taken me on a journey that has enabled me to face and overcome a fear and work through the odd challenge to come through with them changed and much better off.

The local bank manager came to one of our sessions and was extremely encouraging asking to be invited again to address the next group. His words were, "I speak to business groups and honestly I have never seen a group so engaged. "

Each week we would have a discussion around the previous week's lesson and what they had found useful or used, and then the group would get questions ready for the next speaker who was coming to address them. They wanted answers from that speaker too. They asked really good questions and were prepared. We would write the questions on the board and go over them if the speaker hadn't covered that information in their presentation.

Question and answer time with this group is not a courtesy filler at the end of a session it becomes another extension to the session.

Every speaker was impressed with the group and their questions, and the group got better and better at asking questions.

From some questions in the first sessions to many questions in the later weeks their confidence grew and they asked questions about tiny things. Tiny things we don't think about.

We live in a digital world but not everyone has daily access to that digital medium so questions around why, if we phone to get information do we have to wait so long to have it sent to us?

Their thinking is if the organization has the technology they should be able to print the information off and get it posted the same day as they do with an email address.

I forgot to mention earlier despite how these people first presented not one of them is silly. They are intellectually a very savvy bunch indeed.

Each week they would revise and review what they were doing with their money and make small changes. The next week they would share with the group what they had done, what they had found useful and what didn't work.

Things not working out was not a failure it was part of the elimination process of what did not work for them.

Looking at behaviours and their triggers became a huge part of this course.

Why do you go to the shops?

To fill in time.

Are you spending money when you go?

Yes.

Was that your intention when you went?

No I just wanted to fill in time.

Going to the Library or walking to the park has been much more beneficial for financial gain.

Adding to all things for success

What we did as a group was take a risk. Everyone involved including me did this. It worked well, I believe, because we were all honest. When something didn't work we admitted it, looked at why that may not have worked out, let it go and moved on.

Second guessing decisions was not encouraged. Looking at another option was. Having the goal as the focus, whatever that goal was for the person was paramount, and everyone was aware of the goal.

There has been a collaboration that has been truly inspirational and it has been present throughout, in part, I believe, because everyone has been open nonjudgmental, while respecting each other's opinions.

I have titled this chapter small things because it has truly been the small changes in thinking, expectation, bits of new knowledge, and doing things slowly in small steps that has been transformational for the people in this group.

Small things like, take only a five dollar note with you when you buy a bottle of milk and a loaf of bread. The change is not sufficient for you to buy anything else. Put the change in a jar and leave it there.

Using smaller amounts of money in cash and not swiping the EFTPOS card has saved lots of money.

Keeping all your receipts and going over them at the end of the week to see where your money is actually being spent and on what.

Many of the group had just been saying "You keep it or I don't need it." When asked if they wanted their till docket or receipt. Now they are asking for them.

Direct Debits have now been changed for Automatic Payments and those who have made this change feel in control of their money.

The overall achievements

For this group of people, they are now empowered to make decisions about their money. They have a new appreciation of the fact that the money is theirs. They can say no to others who want it. They can choose what they want or need to do with it. They know the difference between need and want. The lines are no longer blurred.

They have learned already that just by putting small amounts aside, they can save huge stress down the line.

This holiday season they are going to track where their money went and on what. Next year we will be doing part two of the course on planning for the year, including preparing for the Christmas season of that year.

Everyone without exception has reduced financial stress in their lives. This has happened in an eight week period. Yes an eight week period and they are all excited about the upcoming sessions next year.

They have family involved and more people wanting to do the course next year so there could well be another rollout of the course again for a new group of people.

All this from a need and small things taking

place.

Small things are what make the greatest difference in our world, its environment and its people.

Just stopping and taking a few minutes a day to enjoy the quiet has exponential benefit to people.

Just a small thing in a busy life.

What this group and their Tutor have learned is that the small things are the very things that have had the most impact overall.

Open honest discussion. Honest self-reflection. Being objective. Evaluating outcomes without guilt. Making changes. Putting bits aside. Planning for the unexpected. Being honest when you say yes or no. If it is a loan it needs to be paid back. If it is a gift give it joyfully. Know the difference.

If a loan is not paid back and the people want more? No I am not a bank.

Those six words have saved lots of money already.

Small things. Big results.

Chapter 10. Promises we make

I was reminded quite some months ago now, that God knows our hearts. Everyone's. Perhaps that's why we have forgiveness available to us? Well the speaker on this occasion had my attention. I had never thought about forgiveness in quite this light.

Moving on to the very recent past and this memory was revisited in a very nice way.

A person won a first division lotto and power ball prize in the millions of dollars. This does happen on occasion for people and I am always pleased and happy for them. Normally you are told very little about the person or their circumstances which is understandable.

Sometimes the person wants the world to know and then finds that years later the world is still knowing what they are doing.

Winning millions of dollars certainly polarizes people in certain directions. Some people expect to be able to just be given some of it because a person has won. Some people just give it all away and that happens often.

Back to my recent winner. I got home from work and my husband told me that the person who won lotto and power ball was going to give half of it to a friend of his who years earlier he had promised that if he ever won lotto he would give him half.

I was filled with joy. It was quite an unsolicited feeling that welled up in me and I said "That's lovely he was definitely the right person to win."

Now there will be many people reading this thinking many different things. You could be thinking that's great, but I could have done with the money. You could be thinking, well he said that but that doesn't mean he will follow through.

Whatever we think, clearly this person made a promise. A promise is a commitment. A commitment is something which requires a follow through. An accountability.

How much thought do you actually give to your promises

Many people make promises. Promises are intentions to do something for yourself or others when you receive something or have achieved something. They don't always relate to money. They can be gifts you have and share. They could be skills you make available to others.

Whatever you have promised though, you need to be sincere when you make the promise, and honest when you are able to deliver on the promise.

One of the issues with promises is the time component. I will give you an example. In 1980 you make a promise to your best friend. In 2020 forty years on, you are in a position to make good on your promise to that person.

Now things may have happened over the forty years, you may no longer be friends with this person so what do you do?

All I am saying here is that when you make a promise, with sincerity and intention you also have to live with the follow through and what you do with it.

Now possibly forty years on you may have lost

touch with the person or you may be living in completely different parts of the world or your country. Your circumstances may be completely different, but when you made the promise you were best friends. You had a bond.

The most amazing things can happen when you least expect them, and technology is a tool of great help these days when you need to reconnect or find people.

Six years ago a very dear friend of mine and she is my oldest friend found me this way. We had been living in different countries for thirty years but we thought of each other often and reminisced often about our younger days together. Our formative years. She happened upon some information then acted on it, and voila we are back in touch with each other and it is as if no time has passed at all.

Excuses won't wash

If you find yourself coming up with old or routine excuses that result in you not following through on a promise you have made, know that you are not fooling anyone.

We have a legal system in the west that will ensure that if you made a promise and it was sincere the other person can take action to receive what you promised them. Now they may not be successful in receiving it, but trust me the financial cost is nothing to what the emotional cost might be. Not to mention the time it may take to sort out.

Then there is the spiritual cost. If you know you just don't want to honour the promise, that the situation between you has changed, or you have grown and gone in a different direction, you need to be very clear about that and ask for protection from your internal counsellor. Other people may see the situation differently.

If you act on your promise however and the other person or people involved say no that was then, this is now, and they no longer want to be a part of the promise, then that is okay as well and depending on the promise that may well be great for them.

I will give you an example. You are in a band in your teens. You play on the weekends for some pocket money. Two of you in the band have dreams of being professional musicians and you make a promise to your fellow musician that when the opportunity arrives you will let him know and continue on your musical way together. You both leave school and get on with your lives. You take different paths. You hear things about your former band mate. He is still playing gigs on the weekend, now has a job and a family, as do you.

Then one day you are performing at a wedding and a guest comes up to you, introduces themselves as an agent and asks if you are interested in a professional music career. You are excited and mention you have a former bandmate you can bring on board as well.

A meeting is arranged and you are on a road trip to see your friend. You are so excited and feeling great that the promise you made can be realised.

You get to your former band mate and share the great news with him and he looks dumb struck. "Thanks but that was then. We were just kids. I love the life I have now so thanks, but no thanks."

"But you still play." You say incredulously.

"Yes I do still play. I play for pleasure now and I love it. It is a great stress release for me and I get paid to do it. It provides the extras that makes my life more comfortable, but it's not my life. I love my career. I love that I have time to spend with my family. If I was a professional musician I would be on the road all the time and missing out on the things I enjoy now. When we were young it was a way of having all we wanted right then, but I have all I want now and I am happy with the choices I've made. Let me ask you why do you want to walk away from everything and be a professional musician now?"

"I have always wanted to be a professional musician. That is what I've worked towards for years."

"Then live your dream and thanks for remembering what you promised me, but I am happy doing what I am doing. I wish you all the best. You know there is no reason why we can't do the odd set together that could be fun."

The way you go forward

As with all things you are the one making the decisions. You made the intention. Yes, a promise is an intention of what you will do when.

You need to decide the way forward when the goods, money or circumstances arrive. You need to make the decision with integrity and be honest with and true to yourself.

Sometimes promises involve unexpected results or actions.

In all things though you are better to do your best as you would in any other situation. If you genuinely try to find someone and are unable to locate them, document what you have done and keep it in a safe place, in case you need to show the actions you have taken.

If you have promised to volunteer for an organization when time permits and you no longer are involved with that organization there is no reason at all why you can't volunteer time for another organization. I say this because the promise may well have been, when I have more time I will do volunteer work, and just because you no longer are with that organization it doesn't mean that you can no longer give time to volunteer.

The excuse may be, I no longer work for the organization, but the promise was time volunteering.

Know what your promise is

When we are young we make promises all the time because we trust things will happen that are good for us.

When we are older we have often learned that things don't always work out the way we see they will through a child's eye.

This is one of the things that we need to correct. We need to trust and believe as a child does. Just ask, then believe to receive.

This is a biblical teaching by the way.

We don't have to worry about the how or the when the timing is always perfect.

So when you make a promise know what your promise is and realise that there may well be a time delay. Not a denial. A delay. Delays can really mix things up when promises are involved. So know what your promise really is. Have a plan for it, so that if there is a time delay you have a plan to manage it, and honour it, or honour the essence, the intention of it.

Years ago a friend of mine was faced with the loss of someone she was very close to. What made it hard was the age of the person. Someone with a life to be lived ahead of him and struck down on the precipice of achievement. My friend had made a promise to help him into a business venture. That sadly did not happen, however my friend decided that the current business opportunity was comfort and quality of what life was left to be lived. She bought him a van, which accommodated his wheelchair as his health and mobility declined, and paid for a driver to get him around.

Every day we have the opportunity to make promises, to break promises, to honour our promises.

It starts and ends with you so make good on
as many of your promises as you can.

I make a promise every day to help someone.
It doesn't have to cost any money, what the
true cost is to do it.

A smile that takes two seconds can uplift
someone. Sharing of skills can encourage and
inform someone. Sharing a few extras can
save someone.

Best of all if you promise to love yourself and
love others you will be in a happier space. The
more you honour that promise the better we
all will be.

Enjoy your promises and remember you may
well receive a blessing beyond your wildest
dreams because someone made a promise.
Right now that is happening to someone as
they receive millions of dollars into their bank
account from a promise made years ago and
now honoured.

Chapter 11. The blessings you never saw coming

I was all set for the summer break and looking forward to weeks of uninterrupted writing. I could see the application going in for another ISBN. I could see the cover of the book being done and the click to add a new book to my growing list and then......

Yes something completely unexpected arrived. A software programme to make my writing across multiple formats, more attainable, and more efficient. In the first instance this will also be more time consuming.

Yes I now had to learn how to use it. So my focus on the writing was still very much there,

but the vehicle had changed somewhat. A bit
like going to the supermarket in a second
hand, overworked, spluttering car, then
driving home having won a brand new Ferrari.
Getting into the Ferrari is an art in itself, but
once seated you turn the key and you are off
literally.

Technology, as I am learning, is something
new, and like all new things, you have to learn
how to use them, but for me I am also
learning that the more of them I learn to use,
the quicker the learning process is becoming
and technology has opened my world up.

I have studied using technology. I have
published using technology. I have helped
many other people through the use of
technology. I keep in touch with family
through technology.

Yes I am older, but I am discovering a whole
new appreciation for technology that I did not
have before.

Why is there such a transformation?

When I was working in my early twenties
technology had just been introduced. It was
so efficient that it efficiently replaced me and
when my maternity leave was up I had no job
to return to, so it is not surprising that my
first brush with technology wasn't a positive

one for me.

Then in my thirties I again got to use technology and found it to be mildly useful. I say mildly useful, because the cost of services was high, and the speed things happened was slow and cumbersome. We used the DOS system and that was in and of itself a challenge for the average Joe Blogs. Push this button for that, and then that button for this, and don't forget to use your arrow keys.....

And here I am in my fifties thinking I would never be proficient in the use of technology and I find myself surrounded by it everywhere, and now embracing it in the sanctity of my writing as well.

Take another look at your everyday things are they now blessings too?

We have been preparing the house for painting with interruptions over two years and now finally my husband is painting the final coats. For many weeks he has been toiling to get things ready for this wondrous moment. Well I see this as a wondrous moment because I have been grateful and thankful for our home being painted and looking amazing for two years.

At the back door of our home we have a frame

which houses the nova lite which keeps the back porch dry and allows light to stream into the dining room in the long dark winter months.

Two days ago the nova lite came off and the frame was undercoated. Yesterday the final coats went on. The climbing up and down the scaffolding, shifting the scaffolding was tiring even me out and I was the observer to the progress.

This morning when my husband got up he stated "I am looking forward to painting the boards of the house."

Just last week he wasn't so keen on doing more boards, having finished a longer side of the house so more progress on the house today.

Sometimes things are not what they seem

Why do things often move to a timeframe different to ours?

I have no idea, but what I have discovered over time is that the timing is always perfect.

This is also true of things. What we desperately want isn't always what we need, and sometimes what we need is also what we want.

Confusing? Life can be, but as we participate with an open mind in life we get to know exactly what we want and need, and they both start turning up, often with extras far beyond what we expect.

I have said it before, a delay is not a denial. Just keep being thankful for all you have now. Keep being thankful for what you want as if you also have it now.

This works, I am seeing my home painted and it looks amazing just as I knew it would. The colour is great, the gloss finish is stunning and sets the front door off. The house is literally drawing people to it. People are stopping and looking at it as they walk past, and we are loving the brightness and vibrancy of our home. We are both even sleeping better.

We love our home and our home is loving the attention and the makeover it is receiving.

Makeovers come in all shapes, sizes and ways

Be honest with yourself today. Ask yourself what is here already that I can make over into something better to bring joy back into my life.

For those of you have read my other books
you will know that my dream house is in
another part of our country nearer to our
family. As you can tell two years on from my
intentions being put out, I am still residing in
the home we are now painting but I am
undeterred. I still see myself walking around
my new home in the Waipa District with the
family visiting, love, laughter, and
companionship abounds, and let's not forget I
have my writing room, which has tulips on the
walls, and yes, another tulip picture has been
acquired for that very purpose. In fact I said
to my husband the other day, we are so lucky,
we have got nearly everything we need for our
next house, so it won't be long now.

In the meantime I am taking another look at
what we do, and what we no longer need and I
am getting ready for the shift. Nothing will
deter my vision. There have been some
glitches, but my vision is absolute just as it
has been with the painting of our current
home. Even my husband is falling in love
with the house, the house seems to be waking
up and looking for new owners, so everything
is coming together.

We tend to think of makeovers these days as
the glossy, glitzy, throw out and replace or
sand down and cover off things, but really
what is a makeover?

For me a makeover comes from within. I have
a makeover on the inside. An attitude
makeover.

Once my attitude is made over it is just
amazing what happens on the outside.

I spent several months being frustrated that
the weather wasn't right. Too cold. Too wet.
Then the weather would be right and the
husband was too tired, too stressed and the
result was nothing happening with the house.
Every day I would come home from work and
see an unfinished house, which is worse for
me than a house that needs to be started.
Then one day I just saw our home finished.
Every day, regardless of what greeted me at
the end of the day I saw my home finished,
then one day I arrived home and the front of
the house was undercoated. Then two days
later the final coats were on the house and the
progress has been phenomenal.

I will say it again never give up

Two years ago I should have had a more
excited more connected attitude to our home
but we have got there now.

I am putting this newfound confirmation of
how things work better with an attitude
makeover to new areas of my life. My job,
which I love and am grateful for, but has been

challenging recently, is also experiencing a makeover. Our next home is getting the makeover treatment as well. I am not getting hung up on the how, the time it is taking, the means to get there, no I am just grateful we are there and it is an amazing property, it comes with established grounds and native birds, just the current home we live in, only the next one is bigger, and we have an amazing life there.

I get goosebumps just thinking about it and seeing it.

If you find yourself in a place where things have not arrived yet, give your attitude a makeover. Look over all the things you currently have. Look at them and see how you can either use them in new ways, appreciate them better or have the courage to let them go from your life making room for new, and more appropriate things to arrive.

Don't second guess yourself. Don't over analyse what you are doing. Just trust in yourself and do.

The scaffolding has moved to another part of the house. I am excited and I encourage you to be excited. Once you get excited, you get connected to the life you want. Keep the excitement alive and never give up.

You know every day we have the amazing gift of being able to start over. Don't let a bad day or a disappointment ruin your journey, get yourself up and do an attitude check, and check in to your good attitude. If it is lacking, then a makeover is in order. Be courageous. You can do it.

Chapter 12. Appreciating the gifts in your basket

As last year has closed and we are now in a New Year I have emptied my receiving basket and gone through all the things I received last year.

What is amazing to me reading through my receipts are all the things I had not asked for that arrived. These additional blessings arrived at the perfect time, and although unexpected served a purpose that I had not foreseen.

They came in many different ways, in person, by courier, by post, by phone, by email, by Skype, through work, all manner of ways they showed up and brought me immeasurable joy.

I also managed to be a blessing or provide unexpected joy to people over the year. A phone call, a smile, a sit down and listen, giving gifts, providing a suggestion or a solution that resulted in a good outcome for people.

My receiving basket did not get a chance to be empty between the 31st of December and the 1st of January.

I physically emptied the basket on the 31st of December at 10.00 p.m., and by 9.00 a.m. on the 1st of January I had a new blessing to put into my receiving basket.

Coincidence? You all know what my thoughts are on that. There is no such thing as coincidence in my world. Everything happens for a reason.

My receiving has increased exponentially since I have put my receiving basket out.

My winnings have increased since I expected to receive winnings.

I have received good people, good things and good experiences since I expected them to arrive.

Every day I ask for them. Every day. Not once in a while. Every day.

No matter what the day may look like it could be, I am focusing on the day I want it to be. I put my head into a place where I am receiving good.

During the everyday stuff

I recently saw my Doctor for a check -up. He asked me what I had been doing as I had lost 3 Kilograms.

"I have been going for the occasional leisurely walk. About an hour at a time. Sometimes forty minutes. I have been writing. I have been doing Tapestry. I stand to write I have a standing desk for that. I stand and do my Tapestry I asked my husband to make me a frame I can stand at. I have been resting. I have not been rushing. I have not been power walking. I have been eating just the same as always. In fact if anything I have slowed down."

"How long would you be standing when you do your writing?" he asked me.

"Two or three hours and about the same when I do my Tapestry."

"It is very unusual for someone to stand and do those things. How can you stand for that long?"

"I have my mind occupied so I am not thinking about standing. When I am doing Tapestry I am usually watching a DVD at the same time, listening to music, or on speaker phone to someone. My mind is actively engaged. When I am writing I am thinking about what I am writing. I stand because when I am at work in front of a group of people I am standing, so the more I stand the easier it is when I am working."

The great thing about standing so much is that when I sit down to relax I do just that. I sit. I relax.

Be aware of your every day

Be intentional every day. Start your day with the thoughts of how you want it to be. Now it may not work out that way in the beginning, but with practice your intentions have expectation attached to them, and those two things are a formidable combination.

I now start my day this way every day.

"Dear God please fill me with your holy spirit to over flowing. I am asking that something good happen to me today. I am asking that something good happen through me today. (For others.) I am asking that I receive good news today."

At the end of my day I write in my journal what has happened to me, through me and what good news I have received that day, and every day I see my prayers being answered.

Now you may be thinking it is such a little thing why bother asking for it, it would probably have happened anyway.

Or you may be thinking God won't do that for me, or I wouldn't ask God for that.

Here's the thing I have learned. If I want something, big or small is immaterial, I have to first expect it. I have to receive it. I have to see myself with it.

I see myself everyday now receiving something good, doing something good for others and receiving good news. Every day I am blessed with those things, sometimes multiple times through the day.

Creating your shift

"If you want to accomplish something then first you have to expect it of yourself."

When I had the desire to write I had no idea how this was going to happen. I went back to high school to do some business papers and took English as well. It was through my English subject and the essays I wrote that my English teacher said "You have a flair for writing I think you should pursue that."

Less than a month later I saw an advertisement for a Writing Diploma Course through correspondence with the International Writing School. I spoke to my mum who lent me the money to do it, and over the following months I studied and paid her off. By the end of the course I had passed and paid for the course in full.

That course has helped me fulfill the desire I had to be a writer, but it was the confirmation I could write in the first place that gave me the expectation I could be a writer.

 I am a professional writer. That means I have been paid to write. I am a writer. I accomplished that which I knew I could be, and I have learned that I can do this in all areas of my life.

Many times we are put off from stretching ourselves.

How does this come about?

For many years I allowed the opinion of others to affect the way I saw myself. It has taken me many years, life experiences, and new information to change this.

Along the way I have received support, and encouragement from others.

My detractors have fallen away. I have focused and concentrated on my abilities, my desire to help others, and I have continued to read and upskill my knowledge, putting new things that feel right for me into practice.

As I have said many times before, I focus on good things arriving, good things happening for myself and others, good situations appearing, and I see these things before they actually occur.

I am thankful for many things, but I am no longer silent about those things.

I express my thankfulness openly, often and honestly.

What I have found is that I am receiving more things to be thankful for.

Just the other day I stumbled across a book that deals with the theory subject of being the good girl.

The good girl being identified as a woman who is not allowed to express anger, is not expected to express an opinion, is not expected to be aggressive in business, all things that are accepted of male behaviours without question or criticism.

Just because for generations people have expected and accepted those behaviours doesn't make them right.

I had a random thought while I was driving home from work the other day about a saying I would hear often when my sister or I were in a bad mood.

"Go back to bed."

Possibly we were tired. More probably our mother was tired, or tired of our behaviours in that moment. What I know is that once we were back in bed we did not get up until we were told to.

If we think about that saying in our adult life though we can literally take a deep breath, close our eyes, see ourselves going back to bed, breathe deeply a few times then get ourselves up again, with a new focus, a better attitude and continue on with our day.

Going back to bed is not the issue. What we feel when we wake up is.

If we wake up refreshed and ready to embrace our day we will do just that.

I encourage you to embrace every day.

I encourage you to effect positive change in your life.

I encourage you to persist in the life you see for yourself.

I encourage you to get a good team of supporters around you.

It starts with you and you know you can make it happen.

You deserve it. Success is not just for others. It is for you too. It is yours for the taking. Be courageous and start your amazing journey. Enjoy it. I am.

Remember it starts with you and you will reap the benefits.

ABOUT THE AUTHOR

KAREN PIVOTT is the author of *Self Help Books, Adult Fiction and Children's Fiction and is a published radio scriptwriter with HCJB Beyond the Call with Ron Cline series 2001. Radio Southland 2004 and 2005.* Published play write "Gavin's 21st." 2000 Nelson fringe art festival and literacy specialist. Karen lives in Invercargill New Zealand with her husband. Karen loves educating and inspiring people to improve their lives and the lives of all the people they connect with.

www.ingramcontent.com/pod-product-compliance
Lightning Source LLC
Chambersburg PA
CBHW050006070726

47592CB00018B/1071